WOODROW WILSON

The Presidents of the United States

George Washington
1789–1797

John Adams
1797–1801

Thomas Jefferson
1801–1809

James Madison
1809–1817

James Monroe
1817–1825

John Quincy Adams
1825–1829

Andrew Jackson
1829–1837

Martin Van Buren
1837–1841

William Henry Harrison
1841

John Tyler
1841–1845

James Polk
1845–1849

Zachary Taylor
1849–1850

Millard Fillmore
1850–1853

Franklin Pierce
1853–1857

James Buchanan
1857–1861

Abraham Lincoln
1861–1865

Andrew Johnson
1865–1869

Ulysses S. Grant
1869–1877

Rutherford B. Hayes
1877–1881

James Garfield
1881

Chester Arthur
1881–1885

Grover Cleveland
1885–1889

Benjamin Harrison
1889–1893

Grover Cleveland
1893–1897

William McKinley
1897–1901

Theodore Roosevelt
1901–1909

William H. Taft
1909–1913

Woodrow Wilson
1913–1921

Warren Harding
1921–1923

Calvin Coolidge
1923–1929

Herbert Hoover
1929–1933

Franklin D. Roosevelt
1933–1945

Harry Truman
1945–1953

Dwight Eisenhower
1953–1961

John F. Kennedy
1961–1963

Lyndon B. Johnson
1963–1969

Richard Nixon
1969–1974

Gerald Ford
1974–1977

Jimmy Carter
1977–1981

Ronald Reagan
1981–1989

George H. W. Bush
1989–1993

William J. Clinton
1993–2001

George W. Bush
2001–2009

Barack Obama
2009–

WOODROW WILSON

KATIE MARSICO

 **Marshall Cavendish**
Benchmark
New York

Library of Congress Cataloging-in-Publication Data

Marsico, Katie, 1980–
Woodrow Wilson / by Katie Marsico.
p. cm.—(Presidents and their times)
Summary: "Provides comprehensive information on President Woodrow Wilson and places him within
his historical and cultural context. Also explored are the formative events of his times and how he
responded"—Provided by publisher.
Includes bibliographical references and index.
ISBN 978-0-7614-4815-0
1. Wilson, Woodrow, 1856–1924—Juvenile literature.
2. Presidents—United States—Biography—Juvenile literature. I. Title.
E767.M37 2011
973.91'3092—dc22
[B]
2009041116

Editor: Christine Florie
Publisher: Michelle Bisson
Art Director: Anahid Hamparian
Series Designer: Alex Ferrari

Photo research by Thomas Khoo

The photographs in this book are used by permission and through the courtesy of:
alt.type/Reuters: 3, 93, 95 (l); *Corbis:* 25, 35, 47; *Library of Congress:* 37, 39, 50, 77;
Marian Turcan: *National Geographic Society:* 79; *North Wind Picture Archives:* cover, 13, 28,
54, 94 (r); *Topfoto:* 6, 8, 9, 14, 15, 17, 19, 20, 23, 40, 41, 42, 43, 45, 49, 51, 53, 57, 58, 59,
63, 66, 68, 71, 72, 74, 75, 78, 80, 82, 83, 84, 85, 86, 88, 89, 94 (l), 95 (r).

Printed in Malaysia
1 3 5 6 4 2

CONTENTS

Woodrow Wilson served as president from 1913 to 1921.

Minister's Son and Princeton Scholar

"*Sometimes* people call me an idealist," Woodrow Wilson once remarked. "Well, that is the way I know I am an American. America is the only idealistic nation in the world." For the man who would ultimately become the twenty-eighth president of the United States, working tirelessly to ensure that his nation achieved the highest standards of peace, democracy, and international leadership was indeed a major goal. Though the American public often perceived Wilson to be quiet and reserved, he was nonetheless ambitious, passionate, and determined.

He was also frequently unwilling to compromise on issues that he considered to be important. This stubbornness sometimes served him well. On other occasions, however, it created challenges in his political relationships and caused people to view him as unrealistic, uncooperative, and too much of an idealist.

Regardless of how the world thought of him, though, certain facts about Wilson remain undeniable decades after he headed the country. For starters, he was a respected and intelligent scholar who was known for his role as an educational leader at Princeton University, in Princeton, New Jersey. Once he became involved in politics, he also earned a reputation for dedicating himself to government reform and changes that he believed would benefit America and its citizens.

Finally, as president, he desperately struggled to keep the United States out of World War I (1914–1918). When it was clear that the nation could no longer afford to remain neutral, Wilson rallied soldiers, politicians, and average men and women from all walks of life to support the U.S. military effort overseas. Unfortunately, his precise goals for peace and international unity following the war were not all achieved, but he is still remembered for his intense desire to shape America—and the world—into places where ideals had the potential to become realities.

The Childhood of Tommy Wilson

Joseph Ruggles Wilson and Jessie Woodrow Wilson celebrated the birth of their first son, Thomas Woodrow, on December 28, 1856. The couple, who already had two daughters, Marion and Annie, affectionately called the little boy Tommy, though he later wanted to be addressed as "Woodrow." The Wilsons also had a second son, Joseph Junior, born nearly a decade later.

Woodrow Wilson admired his parents Joseph and Jessie.

This home in Staunton, Virginia, is the birthplace of Woodrow Wilson.

Tommy was born in Staunton, Virginia, but his family moved to Augusta, Georgia, while he was still a toddler. His father became a respected pastor of a Presbyterian church there, and the Wilsons' day-to-day life was deeply shaped by prayer, reflection, and religion. It was also inevitably affected by the Civil War (1861–1865), the bloody national conflict that divided the North, or the Union, from the South, or the Confederacy, over the issue of slavery. As an adult, Wilson recalled having seen wounded soldiers pass through town and even remembered catching a glimpse of the Confederate general Robert E. Lee when he came to Augusta. Young Tommy regarded the Southern hero with awe, much in the same way he did his own father.

Tommy admired both his parents and was deeply attached to his family. Since the war and health issues such as severe headaches and indigestion kept him out of school until age thirteen, his mother and father were primarily responsible for his education until that point. Joseph Wilson was especially determined to help his son develop a better understanding of vocabulary and the importance of speaking in an educated, eloquent manner. The lesson was a powerful one that would prove particularly meaningful as Tommy grew up and embarked upon a political career.

"As a young boy . . . even at the age of four or five, I was taught to think about what I was going to say, and then I was required to say it correctly," he later recalled. "Before I was grown, it became a habit." The minister also encouraged Tommy to practice and appreciate the art of debate. Perhaps most importantly, though, he urged the boy to think about how he could change his country and the world for the better.

Though he would one day lead the nation, young Wilson at first struggled academically.

This inspiration was helpful to Tommy, who did not do well academically when—as a teenager—he began attending a local school run by a former Confederate soldier named Joseph T. Derry. While he made a handful of friends with whom he enjoyed playing baseball, he struggled with some classroom subjects, was simply uninterested in others, and had to work hard to master reading and writing. Several historians believe Tommy may have been suffering from **dyslexia**. He was often sick, as well, and so was frequently absent from school.

Tommy's academic record failed to improve when the Wilsons moved to Columbia, South Carolina, in 1870. Instead of focusing on his own coursework, he preferred to observe classes that his father taught at the local theological seminary, where young men were trained to become Presbyterian ministers. Yet his unimpressive performance as a student in no way meant that Tommy lacked intelligence or ambition.

On the contrary, he was a quiet, thoughtful dreamer—an individual strongly guided by religion but one who also spun fantastic tales surrounding the navy and the sea. And, even at a relatively early age, the solemn yet intense teenager managed to make a striking impression on those around him. The boy who would ultimately become the leader of the nation was not identical to so many of the other high-spirited, mischievous young men he met in Columbia.

One of his classmates later remembered Tommy as "extremely dignified" and added, "He was not like other boys. He had a queer way of going off by himself." At first, these tendencies led the Wilsons to suspect that their oldest son was likely to become a clergyman. It appeared that Tommy also felt the same way in the autumn of 1873, when he started attending Davidson College—a Presbyterian school located about twenty miles from Charlotte, North Carolina. By May 1874, however, it was clear that his time there would be brief. Homesick and experiencing severe indigestion, the teen returned to Columbia.

Within months, the Wilson family relocated to Wilmington, North Carolina, where Joseph Wilson accepted another church position. Meanwhile, along the Atlantic waterfront, his eighteen-year-old son daydreamed. Suffering from headaches, poor eyesight, stomach problems, and nervousness, young Wilson found relief in imagining that he would one day enjoy a sailor's life and serve in the U.S. Navy. His mother did not hesitate to discourage such fantasies. Extremely protective of her children, Jessie Wilson feared what might become of her boy on rough seas or in the midst of a naval battle.

Yet her beloved son was nearly twenty by the fall of 1875, and he was eager to pursue a career that would change and improve the world, just as his father had always encouraged him to do. He therefore left Wilmington to enroll in the College of New Jersey; the college was later renamed Princeton University, after the town in which the institution is located. Though Wilson may not have realized it at the time, it was there that he would become deeply fascinated by the American political system that he would ultimately be chosen to lead.

Campus Life and Lively Politics

Unlike Davidson, where most students had focused on training to become Presbyterian ministers, the College of New Jersey was filled with young men pursuing other ambitions. Most of the school's approximately five hundred male attendees came from wealthy backgrounds, and several had fathers or close relatives who were involved in American politics. While Wilson's family life had been largely rooted in religion—and even though he still

Wilson attended the college of New Jersey (now Princeton University) from 1875 to 1879.

remained somewhat unexceptional academically—the atmosphere at the College of New Jersey suited him.

While enrolled there, he further developed his skills as a debater and public speaker. He also started to gain a reputation for being a leader among his fellow students. His classmates named him speaker of the American Whig Society, an organization that concentrated on debating, politics, and literature. He was likewise appointed secretary of the Football Association, president of the Baseball Association, and the managing editor of a college newspaper called *The Princetonian*.

Wilson became a member of the Alligators, as well. This group was one of the campus's eating clubs, which were similar to modern-day fraternities. Such social organizations formed because many early U.S. universities did not offer cafeteria services. The young men who belonged to eating clubs gathered to share meals and enjoy discussions and debates surrounding issues of the day.

Wilson adored these conversations and was particularly drawn to talking about government and politics. Nor was his fascination limited to subjects that strictly related to America. He was also intrigued by foreign governmental institutions, including the habits and structure of Great Britain's **parliament**.

His study of other nations' government systems sometimes led Wilson to question the one in place in the United States. Specifically, he began to believe that the U.S. Congress had too much power and that it did not always act in the best interests of

Wilson (center) with members of the Alligators eating club at the College of New Jersey.

the president or the American people. This suspicion caused Wilson to become swept up in the controversy that took over the College of New Jersey campus during the presidential election of 1876. **Republican** candidate Rutherford B. Hayes was running against **Democrat** Samuel J. Tilden, and the race was filled with complex politics and accusations of corruption. More voters backed Tilden; but in accordance with the Constitution, before the winner of the popular vote can claim victory, he or she must prove to be the strongest candidate in the vote held in the **electoral college**.

In 1876 Hayes won more votes in the electoral college than Tilden. Congress declared that the Republicans had therefore gained control of the White House. Wilson, who supported the Democrats, believed that America's **legislature** had played too

During the 1876 presidential campaign, Republican Rutherford B. Hayes (left) defeated Democrat Samuel Tilden (right).

NOT QUITE THAT QUIET

Some of Wilson's critics noted that he often seemed overly serious and was too quiet. In reality, however, he could become extremely enthusiastic and outspoken when a topic particularly interested him. Politics—and especially debate on the campus of the College of New Jersey surrounding the election of 1876—brought out these reactions in him.

"In consequence of the excitement, which was something over-whelming," he wrote in his journal, "I did no studying in the evening and went to bed . . . tired out with shouting and excitement."

powerful a role in determining the nation's leader after the people had clearly expressed their preference for Tilden. Equal to his disappointment, however, was his excitement over the stir that the election had created on campus. Debates, speeches, and protests at the College of New Jersey transformed politics into a lively subject that Wilson embraced with passion and enthusiasm.

It was his days as a student at the College of New Jersey that helped the minister's son clearly decide what his path in life would be. Wilson would not follow in his father's footsteps by delivering sermons to a Presbyterian congregation—he instead was determined to speak before lawmakers and government officials by establishing himself as a politician. When he graduated in the spring of 1879, he therefore made plans to attend the University of Virginia Law School, in Charlottesville, Virginia.

"The profession I chose was politics," Wilson later explained. "The profession I entered was law. I entered the one because I thought it would lead to the other." The future president was indeed correct about the road he would someday travel after enrolling in law school. It would be several years, however, before Wilson cleared a path toward the White House. Along the way, he was destined to explore other careers and various political perspectives and to experience the joy of falling in love.

This photograph of Woodrow Wilson was taken during his senior year at the College of New Jersey in 1879.

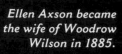

Ellen Axson became the wife of Woodrow Wilson in 1885.

Their relationship would prove an enormous source of strength and happiness to Wilson in the years ahead. "You are the only person in the world—without *any* exception—to whom I can tell *all* that my heart contains," he wrote to her. As Ellen would discover, her suitor's heart was filled with great affection for her and an equally great desire to do something with his life that would change his world for the better.

ADVANCING AS AN EDUCATOR

Wilson wasted little time mapping out a future with Ellen. By September 1883 they were engaged, though they temporarily postponed making detailed wedding arrangements. Ellen was sensible, kind, educated, and extremely talented as an artist. She also seemed to bring about the best in her fiancé. Wilson, however, had only recently decided to abandon the practice of law and return to college to train to become a professor. Having failed to earn any real income during his time in Atlanta, he was unable to provide for a wife and children.

Wilson instead put his efforts into courses he took from 1883 to 1885 at Johns Hopkins University, in Baltimore, Maryland, where he focused on politics and history. These subjects were especially important to him, since he remained determined to one day enter the American political system. Wilson at first experienced the familiar lack of enthusiasm for his studies while attending graduate school in Baltimore. Ultimately, though, he came to enjoy academic life because many of his professors allowed him to work independently and study on his own instead of forcing him to attend lectures constantly. During his time at Johns Hopkins, Wilson also wrote a detailed research paper titled *Congressional Government*.

A Popular, Approachable Professor

While serving as an instructor at the College of New Jersey, Wilson quickly became famous for his enthusiastic lectures and his friendly, approachable manner. Students were not afraid to ask him questions and enjoyed having discussions with him. In turn, he appeared to truly be inspired by his work.

"He had a contagious interest—his eyes flashed," one young man remembered years after having Wilson as his teacher. "I can see him now, with his hands forward, the tips of his fingers just touching the table, his face earnest and animated." Another student recollected, "He talked to us in the most informal, jolly way, yet with absolute clearness and sureness."

"It is indispensable, it seems to me, if [a college] is to do its right service, that the air of affairs should be admitted to all its classrooms," Wilson explained during his address, which was titled "Princeton in the Nation's Service." "I do not mean the air of party politics, but the air of the world's transactions—the consciousness of the solidarity of the race, the sense of the duty of man toward man, of the presence of men in every problem, of the significance of truth for guidance, as well as for knowledge. . . . We dare not keep aloof and closet ourselves while a nation comes to its maturity. The days of glad expansion are gone; our life grows tense and difficult; our resource for the future lies in careful thought, providence, and a wise economy; and the school must be of the nation."

Princeton's most popular professor managed to live out the message of his speech as his career at the university progressed. He urged his students to carefully consider the issues that affected America and encouraged them to look beyond their textbooks for solutions to many of the country's problems. To much of the world around him, he was an unquestionable success. Yet Wilson was never one to remain satisfied with his achievements indefinitely. He knew how to work long and hard to accomplish what he wanted, but he rarely spent much time simply enjoying the rewards of his labor.

As U.S. citizens inched closer to the twentieth century, a great deal was happening in the world that was shaping the nation. For example, the United States was becoming more involved in international affairs. In the Spanish-American War (1898), U.S. forces helped the Caribbean island of Cuba win its independence from Spain. Many people, including Wilson, embraced such efforts with excitement and enthusiasm. They believed that it was time for America, which by then was more than a hundred years old, to take its place alongside other more established countries and enjoy a role in world affairs.

Though Wilson was not yet an actual politician, he was eager to be given every opportunity to do what he had talked about in his speech of 1896—help Princeton serve the nation. Much to his delight, he was given that chance in 1902, when he was appointed president of the university. Wilson immediately prepared to make Princeton one of America's most exceptional places of learning and achievement. To fulfill this goal, however, he also planned a series of reforms that would ultimately spark both progress and varied opinions about his leadership of the university.

In 1902 Wilson was appointed president of Princeton University.

THE POLITICS OF PRINCETON AND BEYOND *Three*

From the start of his presidency at Princeton, Woodrow Wilson made it clear that he had serious ambitions for the college and its student body. If he had his way, the university would not merely be a school where wealthy families could send their sons to socialize at eating clubs and attend parties. Wilson wanted to educate a generation of young men who would be thinkers and active citizens. He hoped that Princeton graduates would go on to change America for the better, just as his own father had urged him to do from an early age.

THE LOSS OF A LIFELONG FRIEND AND COMPANION

Despite his appointment to Princeton's presidency, 1902 was not an entirely happy year for Wilson. Joseph Wilson had begun suffering from a hardening of his blood vessels in 1901, and he grew sicker as time progressed. His wife, Jessie Wilson, had passed away in 1888, and the minister eventually came to live with his elder son in Princeton.

By the end of 1902 it was clear that Wilson's remaining parent was in the last stages of his life. He died on January 21, 1903. Wilson, who had always respected and admired his father, was devastated by the loss. Shortly after his death, he wrote to an acquaintance how he deeply mourned his "life-long friend and companion."

In order to accomplish his plans, Wilson asked the college's trustees to give him $12.5 million for various renovations and reforms. But, while administrators admired his spirit and determination, the funds Wilson had requested represented a significant amount of money—especially during that period in U.S. history. As a result, Princeton's president soon realized that he would perhaps have to move more slowly than he preferred and without all the financial support he had hoped for.

Nevertheless, Wilson was extremely dedicated to making the university one of the best in the nation. He reasoned that one way to do this was to focus on academics and to raise professors' expectations of students. For instance, Wilson believed that Princeton should have stricter admission standards. He did not think it was right for young men to be accepted simply because they came from wealthy backgrounds or had the right social connections. He instead thought that students needed to prove themselves academically and that they should be responsible for continuing to work hard once admitted.

Though the tougher atmosphere at Princeton at first caused a decrease in enrollment, Wilson was not trying to make life miserable for students. In fact, he did a great deal to ensure that only the best learning opportunities were available. For example, he hired additional staff and formed new academic departments. Wilson also remembered how boring he had found many of the lectures he had sat through in his own college days. He therefore hired special assistant professors to help guide students with their reading and to lead them in discussions in small groups.

"We want to transform thoughtless boys into thinking men," he proclaimed during his early years as president. "It should not be our purpose to make the undergraduates work all of the time, but rather to make them *want* to work all of the time. I believe I know this can be done by making the subjects interesting to the men, by getting the men on the inside of them and throwing them on their own resources. I believe there must come in this country a radical change in the system of education." Yet, though several people praised Wilson for his efforts geared toward improving education, not everyone agreed with all his proposals.

CONTROVERSIES ON CAMPUS

Starting in 1906 a heated controversy arose over Wilson's desire to get rid of Princeton's eating clubs. Although he himself had belonged to an eating club as a student, he believed that the groups had become too powerful an influence in day-to-day college life. In his opinion, they encouraged snobbishness and often discriminated against young men who came from less wealthy backgrounds. He regarded Princeton's eating clubs as an example of the social injustice he would later oppose as leader of the nation.

As an alternative to the eating clubs, Wilson suggested that the campus be divided into four rectangular areas called quadrangles. He envisioned each quadrangle having dormitories and cafeterias. While some school administrators applauded Wilson's ideas, many Princeton graduates—alumni—angrily protested. They argued that he was robbing students of their right to freely socialize and that he was threatening to destroy a college tradition that they had once enjoyed. Certain alumni even threatened to stop making donations to the school if Wilson's wishes were carried out.

In the end, the thought of losing money caused administrators to rule against the president's desires. A few university officials suggested compromises that might have addressed some of Wilson's concerns about social inequality on campus without completely abolishing the eating clubs. Ultimately, however, he refused to budge on his insistence that the clubs be absolutely eliminated. Wilson would often demonstrate the same personality trait years later when he was involved in U.S. politics. He was frequently stubborn to the point of sacrificing overall success if it did not match his ideas in every particular detail.

Nor was the presence of the eating clubs the only topic that stirred disagreement between Wilson and Princeton's administrators and alumni. Princeton's president had his mind set on having the graduate school constructed at the center of the campus. On the other hand, Andrew West, the dean of the university's graduate program, believed that the new facility would be better positioned farther away from undergraduate buildings. Wilson argued that the central location would inspire students to work harder during their early college years and make them want to pursue additional educational opportunities. West, however, predicted that the social activities connected with life on campus would distract the young Princetonians enrolled in the graduate school.

The disagreement between West and Wilson grew bitter, with alumni and faculty taking sides and attempting to use donations to persuade administrators that one location was better than another. In May 1910 Woodrow Wilson lost the battle. An alumnus died and left a will granting the university a great deal of money to build the graduate school on the site West wanted.

By that point, Wilson had headed the college for approximately eight years. During that time, he had become increasingly tired of fighting with administrators who were, he felt, too heavily influenced by the financial contributions of the university's graduates. Besides, his first ambition had not been to spend his entire career behind ivy-covered walls. He had once been determined to serve his country as a politician, and that goal continued to appeal to him.

The idea of Wilson involved in U.S. politics intrigued other parties, as well. James Smith Jr., head of New Jersey's Democratic Party, and New York newspaperman and politician George Harvey urged him to abandon life at Princeton. They assured him that a more promising future lay ahead if he would consider running in the upcoming election for the governorship of New Jersey.

Though Smith and Harvey had ambitions of their own that stopped well short of backing an advance by Wilson all the way to the White House, the college president perceived their encouragement as evidence that the nation was ready for new leaders with fresh ideas. He believed they "recognized the fact that a new day had come in American politics." Wilson was committed to playing a role in this exciting era and therefore accepted the Democratic nomination for governor in September 1910.

At Last, a Leader Has Come!

In reality, Smith and Harvey did not focus on Wilson because they thought he would be the best candidate to serve the people of New Jersey. They, along with James Nugent, another Democratic politician from the state, wanted an inexperienced candidate who would bend to their wishes. The trio was deeply connected to **machine politics** in New Jersey's Essex county and Newark.

Smith, Harvey, and Nugent had assessed Wilson as a man who would serve their own purposes. They were confident that he would prove to be a popular candidate who, once elected, would allow them to control the state government. As a result, they did everything in their ability to see to it that he won the Democratic nomination to run in the race for governor. They might not have pushed quite so hard had they known how independent Wilson actually was and how dedicated he would reveal himself to be when it came to furthering his personal political plans.

During his campaign, he called for a "revival of the power of the people." He also promised that, if elected governor, he would fight for stronger government regulation, or control, of utilities and businesses. Wilson believed that, without such efforts, gas, electric, and railroad companies would grow too powerful. Certain utility and transportation businesses were tied into so much wealth and so many corrupt political connections that they quickly eliminated any competition. Under such conditions, the companies remaining were said to hold **monopolies.**

Wilson worried that businesses with monopolies on certain goods and services in New Jersey would both charge outrageous rates and fail to treat their workers properly. While at Princeton, he had seen firsthand how money played a part in deciding many important issues. He did not believe that this was always fair or practical.

Wilson frequently kept these attitudes in mind during his political career as he ran for various offices as part of America's **Progressive movement.** Progressives gained recognition in the late 1800s and early 1900s when they demanded reforms that included stricter government regulation of businesses and utilities. People who were in favor of the Progressive movement opposed monopolies and supported increased workers' rights. They also wanted to grant U.S. voters a greater voice in political affairs. Progressives were greatly opposed to the existing constitutional provision that state legislatures elected senators and other officials who were supposed to represent the people.

As he battled to win the highest office in the state, Wilson proclaimed his support of the Progressive movement. He emphasized over and over that he would rid New Jersey of political and economic corruption, which hurt its citizens. He also publicly stated that he refused to make any promises that would stop him from doing his best to serve the people.

Despite this pledge, local machine bosses had no doubt that they could one day use Wilson as their puppet and so worked hard to ensure that he was elected. In November 1910 their efforts paid off: their candidate became governor of New Jersey after winning approximately 234,000 votes—which was 49,000 more ballots than his Republican opponent, Vivian Lewis, received. Although it would be another two years before Wilson would find his

Wilson delivers a speech to supporters during his campaign for governor.

way to the White House, a growing number of Americans already saw in the fifty-three-year-old former professor the makings of an impressive leader.

"The personal magnetism of the man, his winning smile, so frank and sincere, the light in his gray eyes . . . the beautiful rhythm of his vigorous sentences held the men . . . breathless under their mystic spell," remarked New Jersey politician Joe Tumulty after hearing Wilson speak in 1910. "Men all about me cried in a frenzy, 'Thank God, at last, a leader has come!'"

New Jersey Governor and National Leader *Four*

*B*y 1911 Governor Woodrow Wilson had already gained a reputation as a respected scholar and a Progressive politician. Yet fame did not always mean a life of luxury. For example, to fulfill his duties, Wilson had to go to Trenton, the capital of New Jersey, on every working day. The twenty-two-mile round trip was necessary because the state provided no official governor's mansion, and therefore the Wilsons continued to live in their home in Princeton.

While Wilson's dedication to serving the people of New Jersey was obvious and impressive to many Americans, it failed to win over everyone. It did not take long for George Harvey, James Smith Jr., and James Nugent to recognize that they had little control over the new governor. Since these party bosses had mainly supported the former university president because they believed he would help them further their own political careers, they were bitter and furious when he made decisions that did not agree with their plans.

For starters, Wilson backed Smith's competitor, James Martine, when the two men competed for a seat in the U.S. Senate. The governor preferred Martine and realized that other Democratic politicians in New Jersey favored him, as well. Smith ultimately failed to convince the state legislature that he was a better candidate than his opponent, and he was certain that Wilson's lack of support had played a role in his defeat.

Nugent experienced similar disappointment when the governor chose another politician to replace him as chairman of New Jersey's Democratic Party. He did little to hide his frustration with Wilson and even called him an "ingrate and a liar" shortly before he was stripped of his chairmanship in the summer of 1911. Nugent and machine bosses like him vowed revenge on the man they had so heartily encouraged to run for office just the year before. They threatened that Wilson's political career would suffer as a result of what they called his disloyalty. The governor, however, did not flinch. He was far too busy trying to reform the state by introducing a number of Progressive policies.

For the most part, Wilson succeeded at accomplishing his goals for New Jersey. He got the legislature to support workers' compensation. This program involved the state-funded benefits to individuals who were hurt or injured while performing their jobs.

Wilson fought for the rights of factory workers such as the ones shown here.

Wilson understood that the owners of several big businesses were frequently more concerned with making a profit than with protecting their employees. Some failed to provide safe working conditions for the men and women on their payroll. If an employee had an accident that left him crippled or unable to carry out his responsibilities, company owners often simply replaced that person as he attempted to recuperate from the injury. Workers' compensation guaranteed that the families of salaried workers would not fall into poverty as a result of injury to the breadwinner.

Wilson made sure that the state government did a better job of regulating the rates set by utility companies and railroads, too. Even if the big businesses that controlled gas, electricity, and train transportation held monopolies or had little competition in New Jersey, he was determined not to allow them to charge unfair prices. Wilson was also committed to reshaping the state's election process to better serve the people, and so he created **primaries**. Wilson's efforts to reform New Jersey did not go unnoticed, and, in the spring of 1911, newspaper columnist George Record summed up what many Americans had begun to feel about the governor's positive impact on the state: "The present legislature ends its session with the most remarkable record of progressive legislation ever known in the political history of this or any state," he remarked in one column. "[Without Wilson], nothing of substantial importance would have been passed."

For his part, Wilson wrote in April 1911 about the pride and satisfaction he had experienced while in office: "[I am] quietly and deeply happy that I should have been of just the kind of service I wished to be to those who elected and trusted me." Nevertheless, the governor had not fulfilled the expectations of everyone. The party bosses who were dissatisfied with him

As governor, Wilson pushed for government regulation of rates set by the railroad industry.

were driven to try to cut short his political career. As Wilson would soon prove, however, they were destined to be disappointed once again.

PLANNING A NEW POLITICAL ADVENTURE

Luckily for Wilson and the New Jersey residents who benefited from his reforms, the governor was an ambitious statesman who was extremely dedicated to seeing his political plans achieved. If he had been less determined, the majority of his goals would have gone unaccomplished. Toward the end of 1911, local machine bosses such as Smith and Nugent worked against Progressive Democrats hoping to win seats in New Jersey's legislature. They were eager to withhold their support from any cause or candidate that Wilson favored.

These men also did not believe in all the sweeping reforms suggested by Progressive politicians. As a result of party bosses' unwillingness to fight for a legislature controlled by Democrats, Republican candidates were ultimately able to overtake the New Jersey Senate and General Assembly. By early 1912, therefore, Wilson found himself struggling more and more to get the state legislature to agree with his plans and ideas.

Yet he still was popular among New Jersey residents—and increasingly among Americans across the country. In reality, Wilson's supporters had been encouraging him to think about a run for the U.S. presidency almost as soon as he became governor. At first, he had not taken such suggestions seriously. He had always wanted to serve his nation as a politician, but he actually had far greater experience on college campuses than in government offices. Nevertheless, he had accomplished a great deal in a very short period after being elected governor. As a result, even before 1912, he had gained a network of advisers and political allies who were determining the best strategies for winning the White House.

Businessman William Gibbs McAdoo supported Wilson's run for the presidency.

Tennessee businessman William Gibbs McAdoo was one such supporter. He would also eventually become Wilson's son-in-law when he married Eleanor Wilson, in

1914. Texan Edward Mandell House, also known as Colonel House, was another. A wealthy businessman who had a passionate interest in politics, he would prove to be a trusted friend and counselor during Wilson's career in Washington, D.C. In the meantime, however, House played an important role in helping Wilson gain popularity and the nomination for the presidency on the Democratic ticket, which the party planned on deciding in June 1912 in Baltimore.

Edward Mandell House was friend and counselor to Wilson during his presidency.

A FAMILIAR LEADER

Wilson was pleasantly surprised by Americans' affection for him when he began traveling across the country in 1911 to win popularity with voters in anticipation of the 1912 election. He had not been actively involved in politics long enough to be overly confident. As a result, many people admired his honesty and were pleased that he did not appear to be full of himself or preoccupied by his own success.

"Wherever I go, they seem to like me," he remarked in the spring of 1911. "Men of all kinds and classes. . . . [It is] astounding to find how they have watched me . . . and how well they know me. They received me as they would a familiar leader."

When the Democrats gathered to select their candidate, their choice was far from clear-cut. Wilson had demonstrated his abilities to pass a good deal of Progressive legislation in New Jersey, but not every politician who came to Baltimore in the summer of 1912 believed in Progressive ideals. In addition, the governor had succeeded in making political enemies, especially among machine bosses and their friends.

When the moment arrived for the Democrats to vote, James Beauchamp Clark, Speaker of the U.S. House of Representatives, managed to win more ballots than Wilson. Yet he failed to gain

Wilson was selected as the Democratic candidate to run for the presidency at the 1912 Democratic National Convention.

the support of two-thirds of the delegates, which was necessary to claim the presidential nomination. Wilson had approximately one-third of the vote. In the end, William Jennings Bryan—who had served as the Democratic candidate in 1896, 1900, and 1908—helped decide the issue.

A respected statesman, Bryan believed in many of the reforms that Progressives wanted to see enacted across the nation. He was convinced that Wilson was most likely to make this Democratic vision of change a

Lawyer and political leader William Jennings Bryan helped Wilson secure the presidential nomination.

reality. Bryan therefore announced that he was backing the New Jersey governor. He also influenced several other important national figures to do the same. Wilson therefore captured the two-thirds vote and the nomination. It had been twenty years since a Democratic president had led the country, and the party had high hopes for their fifty-five-year-old candidate, who was joined by vice presidential running mate Thomas R. Marshall.

As Wilson prepared to fight for the highest office in the United States, he had mixed feelings about the journey ahead. On the one hand, he was as determined and ambitious as ever to use his education, talent for public speaking, and willingness to work hard to serve his nation. On the other, however, he already realized that the presidency would be far from simple and would likely take a great toll on his entire existence.

"The next president of the United States," he wrote to a friend in 1912, "would have a task so difficult as to be heartbreaking and . . . I'd probably sacrifice my life to it if I were elected." As the race began, though, Wilson rose to the occasion. He was ready and willing to battle for the opportunity to accept the ultimate challenge in his career.

WINNING THE WHITE HOUSE

Although the Democrats considered their presidential nominee to be very promising, Wilson was not guaranteed victory in the 1912 election. Despite his eloquence as a public speaker and his talk of several reforms that were appealing to average Americans, some voters saw him as too cold and somber. On the other hand, many U.S. citizens regarded Wilson as a noble figure, uninterested in political glory for himself. They looked on him as a man who could help make the United States a more just and modern country, able to take the lead in shrinking the great divide between the rich and powerful and those who were less wealthy.

Luckily for Wilson, other factors in the 1912 race were also in his favor. The most important of these was a lack of unity in the opposing party. Former president Theodore Roosevelt, who had tried and failed to gain the Republican nomination, decided to run as a third-party candidate. In so doing, he pulled support away from the man actually chosen by the Republicans, the incumbent president, William Howard Taft. Unhappy that the Republicans had selected Taft to run again, Roosevelt formed what became known as the Progressive Party.

Like many Progressive Democrats, including Wilson, members of Roosevelt's new party vowed to fight government

Wilson along the presidential campaign trail in New York City in 1912.

corruption and the unfair labor and economic practices of several
of the era's big businesses. The idea of such reforms, popular
though they were with some Americans, was radical and fright-
ening to others. Not every Democrat believed in all the changes
that Wilson spoke of. Unlike Taft, however, Wilson had the
backing of his entire party during the campaign period. Roosevelt
managed to take only a fraction of Republican voters when he ran
as a Progressive. Yet his departure was enough to cripple the
Republican Party in 1912, and neither he nor Taft had enough
support to beat Wilson at the ballot box in November of that year.

The New Jersey governor, however, received the votes of 6.3 million Americans, representing nearly 42 percent of the ballots cast. Roosevelt trailed with 4.1 million votes, and Taft claimed only 3.5 million. Wilson enjoyed an even greater victory in the electoral college, where 435 electors backed him.

The final votes were counted on November 5, 1912. By about 10:00 p.m., Ellen Wilson received a phone call that confirmed her husband's triumph. Serious as ever, Wilson realized that, within a few short months, he would be faced with the duty of leading the entire nation. When he addressed a crowd of hundreds that had gathered outside his family home in Princeton, he explained that he fully understood the huge commitment that would be required of him.

"I have a feeling of solemn responsibility," he declared. "I know that a great task lies ahead of the men associated with me and ahead of myself. Therefore, I look upon you almost with the pleas that you with your thoughts, your best purpose, your purest impulses, will stand behind me and . . . the generous men of the new administration." It would not be the last time that Wilson called upon the American people for their support. In the days and years that followed, both he and they would discover exactly how great a task indeed lay ahead of him.

EARLY DAYS IN OFFICE

Five

From the earliest days of his presidency, Woodrow Wilson demonstrated that he was determined to work hard and accomplish all the changes he had discussed during his campaign. He was far more interested in addressing the various issues that faced the nation than enjoying the electoral victory he had recently experienced. When he was sworn into office on March 4, 1913, he emphasized that it was not a moment of celebration so much as it was a time to begin reforming America and bringing positive changes to the lives of all its citizens.

Woodrow Wilson makes his inaugural address on March 4, 1913.

"This is not a day of triumph," he noted in a speech he gave to crowds that had gathered in Washington, D.C. "It is a day of dedication. . . . Men's hearts wait upon us, men's lives hang in the balance; men's hopes call upon us to say what we will do. Who shall live up to the great trust? Who dares fail to try?" Wilson quickly proved that he was committed to trying his absolute best—and that he also expected Congress to do the same.

Within one month of taking office, the new president had already called members of the U.S. legislature to a special meeting. Up to that time in American history, few presidents personally appeared before Congress, but Wilson was an exception. He wanted to be present to talk to lawmakers about the various reforms he hoped to pass within the next eighteen months.

Among these changes was a reduction in **tariffs**. Wilson was eager for the United States to become more involved in international business and politics, and taxes on goods imported from other countries stood in the way of his vision. On the assumption that tariffs discouraged trade with overseas nations, he urged Congress to pass the Underwood-Simmons Tariff Act. This legislation, which became effective in October 1913, reduced taxes on items shipped to America from abroad.

Yet, even before the Underwood-Simmons Tariff Act was passed, Wilson had realized that the loss of revenue from tariffs would inevitably result in decreased income for the U.S. government. He and Congress had to figure out a way to make up for this loss. Wilson therefore gave his full approval to the Sixteenth Amendment to the U.S. Constitution, ratified in early 1913. The amendment allows the government to collect income taxes from citizens based upon the amount of money they receive each year.

Who Counseled the Country's Leader?

Who was responsible for advising Wilson on matters of state? Like other presidents before and after him, he relied on his cabinet for suggestions and information regarding important issues. In addition to counseling Wilson, members of his cabinet also headed various government departments.

For example, Williams Jennings Bryan initially acted as his secretary of state. Early on in Wilson's presidency, his son-in-law William Gibbs McAdoo was secretary of the treasury. Yet Wilson did not look to his staff alone for input. Colonel House, who never held an official position in Wilson's cabinet, was a friend and trusted adviser up until 1919.

Woodrow Wilson was one of few presidents to appear before Congress.

These measures represented only a portion of Wilson's plans for reform. He addressed the nation's banking system, too. In December 1913, he signed the Federal Reserve Act into law. This legislation created the Federal Reserve System, or "the Fed," which serves as the country's central bank. Wilson believed the Fed was necessary to help stabilize the American economy. Even in the twenty-first century, this government agency continues to play an important role in national finances by continuing to supervise banks across the United States and to regulate interest rates and currency. Interest rates are fees people pay on funds they borrow, and currency is the paper money and coins that are produced by the government.

Wilson also concentrated on efforts to ensure that the country's big businesses operated fairly and that smaller companies had the opportunity to grow and compete with them. In keeping with these ideals, he encouraged Congress to draft the legislation that became known as the Clayton Antitrust Act, passed in October 1914. In addition to protecting laborers' rights, this act

A political cartoon from 1913 satarizes Wilson's currency message to Congress which resulted in the passage of the Federal Reserve Act.

was designed to discourage the formation of monopolies. Another measure that became law in 1914, the Federal Trade Commission Act, allows the president to appoint the members of a governmental agency called the Federal Trade Commission (FTC), which is responsible for monitoring many of the business practices of large companies.

In numerous ways, these reforms made Wilson's first few years in office an incredibly productive and impressive period. As in the early part of his career as New Jersey's governor, he accomplished much of what he wanted. He also did a great deal to improve life for many of the citizens he served. This did not mean, however, that all Americans were satisfied by Wilson's decisions or that controversy never arose as a result of them.

SUFFRAGE AND SEGREGATION

The new president appeared to be a man who—when he was intent on accomplishing a goal—indeed accomplished it. Unfortunately, not all his ambitions for positive change seemed to include *every* U.S. citizen. Women and African Americans were two groups that often felt especially ignored or ill treated as a result of Wilson's policies.

Since the mid–1800s, female citizens who were part of what was known as the **suffrage movement** had been fighting to win the right to vote in presidential elections. At that time, women held a much different place in society than they do today. Some had college educations and successful careers, but many were raised to obey their husbands, fathers, and brothers. Several Americans believed that it was far better for ladies to worry about cooking, cleaning, raising children, and running the household than becoming involved in business and politics.

Unsurprisingly, not every woman in the United States thought she was unqualified to vote. Members of the suffrage movement were determined to win a constitutional amendment that would grant them the right to vote in national elections and thereby have a greater voice in important issues that affected the country. They looked to Wilson with high hopes that, as a new head of state, he would take them seriously. Famous suffragists, including Alice Paul, attempted to gain Wilson's attention by staging a huge parade in the nation's capital to coincide with the arrival of the president-elect in Washington, D.C., for his inauguration in March 1913.

Wilson, however, was not initially interested in going out of his way to battle for a constitutional amendment alongside women who were eager to win the vote. For one thing, the attitudes he had once expressed about female intelligence while he was teaching at Bryn Mawr were not completely changed. In addition, he did not consider suffrage to be as monumental an issue as many of the other topics he was soon to take before Congress. Finally, a

Women march in a parade to support the suffrage movement in Washington, D.C., in 1913.

large number of politicians were not in favor of granting women the right to step up to ballot boxes in national elections.

For all these reasons, Wilson was willing to occasionally talk to suffragists such as Alice Paul and Carrie Chapman Catt, but he urged them to wait patiently. He told them it would be better for the issue to be decided by individual state legislatures before the U.S. government considered an actual constitutional amendment. The president hinted that he was not totally opposed to suffrage but clearly was not willing to give it his full support during his first term in office.

Carrie Chapman Catt frequently discussed her views on suffrage with Wilson throughout his presidency.

"The whole art and practice of government consists not [of] moving individuals but [of] moving masses," Wilson stated at a meeting for suffragists in 1916. "It is all very well to run ahead and beckon, but, after all, you have got to wait for the body to follow. I have not come to ask you to be patient, because you have been, but I have come to congratulate you that there was a force behind you that will beyond any [doubt] be triumphant and for which you can afford a little while to wait."

Part of Wilson's opinions on giving women the right to vote may be traced back to his youth in the South. For the most part, southerners were against woman suffrage. They also were generally opposed to granting African Americans the same rights and privileges as white citizens. Some men and women in the South and in other parts of the country still recalled the days when black slaves worked in their fields and elsewhere on their plantations. Although African Americans had been free for generations, they continued to struggle against racist attitudes and segregation in jobs, education, and other areas of day-to-day life.

Wilson believed that slavery had been wrong, but he was not convinced that whites and blacks should have the same opportunities. He therefore allowed members of his cabinet who headed various government departments such as the Treasury and the navy to segregate their offices. This ultimately meant that African Americans often experienced discrimination when applying for jobs with the federal government. And, those who managed to get hired frequently did not receive fair pay or treatment once on the job.

While some people therefore perceived Wilson as a racist, he insisted that it was not his intention to rob African Americans of their rights or to display any prejudice. He argued that allowing the men in his cabinet to segregate their offices was more likely to create a peaceful, productive work environment. In his mind, keeping blacks separate from whites decreased the risk of conflict between the two groups.

"The purpose of these measures was to reduce the friction," he explained. "It is as far as possible from being a movement against the Negroes. I sincerely believe it to be in their interest."

As the years passed, Wilson's attitudes toward women and people of other races gradually changed. In the meantime, though, he was challenged by new dilemmas both in his own family and across the U.S.-Mexican border.

A WIDOWER FACED WITH WAR

When the Wilsons first entered the White House, they seemed to create one happy family memory after another. Daughters Jessie and Eleanor married in 1913 and 1914, and their elder sister, Margaret, excitedly prepared to train as a professional singer. Meanwhile, Mrs. Wilson did what she had always done so well—supported her husband and used her own intelligence and open-mindedness to encourage him to display the same qualities to the American people.

Sadly, the president would not share much time with his beloved Ellen in Washington, D.C. In 1914 she contracted Bright's disease, a serious kidney ailment that claimed her life on August 6, 1914. Wilson had been in office a little more than a year, and the loss overshadowed any joy he had realized as a result of winning the presidency.

"God has stricken me almost beyond what I can bear," he wrote to a friend shortly after his wife's death. Yet Wilson knew that he would somehow have to bear it, for international crises were erupting all around him. No matter how much he was struggling personally, the nation needed its president to cope with urgent diplomatic situations.

Even before Wilson had been sworn into office, political tension had been building in Mexico. A dictator named Victoriano Huerta had taken control of the government there. In the spring

of 1914, he imprisoned U.S. soldiers in Tampico, which is located on the Gulf of Mexico. Since Huerta's assumption of power, Wilson had quietly but eagerly hoped that revolutionary reformer Venustiano Carranza would seize authority from him.

Yet the president proceeded carefully. Wilson waited for precisely the right moment to oppose Huerta with military troops. The dictator's treatment of American sailors provided the ideal opportunity. With Wilson's help, Carranza was able to gain leadership of Mexico by July 1914. Both men would soon discover, however, that this maneuver did not mean an end to political

U.S. military presence was evident in Veracruz, Mexico, in 1914.

Wilson hoped that another leader would wrestle control of Mexico from the dictator Victoriano Huerta.

difficulties in Mexico. Carranza's government remained unstable, and new revolutionaries, such as the infamous Pancho Villa, led armed raids as a way of demanding additional reforms. In the years following 1914, these attacks would occasionally spill onto U.S. soil, costing Americans their lives and forcing Wilson to continue to involve the United States in Mexico.

Ultimately, though, it was events overseas—and not south of the border—that would truly test the U.S. president's leadership abilities. For, a mere two days before Wilson lost his beloved Ellen, a war like no other began in Europe. On August 4, 1914, the Great War, which later became known as World War I, erupted. The fighting that resulted reshaped how Americans and men and woman all over the world viewed armed conflict.

TROUBLED TIMES FOR THE TWENTY-EIGHTH PRESIDENT

World War I continues to be remembered for some of the deadliest military clashes in history. The fighting lasted four years and claimed more than 15 million lives. The nations that opposed one another poured all their economic, social, and industrial resources into the conflict, throwing soldiers and civilians alike into a period of violence and chaos.

The causes of World War I lay in a series of ongoing rivalries and disputes between various European powers that dated back to the late 1800s. Actual warfare was set in motion in the summer of 1914 with the assassination of Archduke Franz Ferdinand, who was heir to the throne of Austria-Hungary. Following this murder, hostilities intensified between two groups of countries called the **Allied forces**—which at first included Britain, France, Belgium, Serbia, Montenegro, and Russia—and the **Central powers**—initially Germany and Austria-Hungary.

Other nations, including the United States, would ultimately take sides and join in the conflict, as well. During the early stages of the fighting, however, President Woodrow Wilson was determined that America should remain neutral. It was true that he wanted his country to gain a greater voice in international affairs, but he did not want this to occur at the price of U.S. involvement in a large-scale war. Like countless men and women of his generation across the globe, he had never before witnessed such dramatic and far-reaching hostilities. Wilson therefore initially wanted the United States to be a peacemaker, if indeed the country were to play any role in the Great War.

"The effect of the war upon the United States will depend upon what American citizens say and do," he declared during an address to Congress in August 1914. "Every man who really loves America will act and speak in the true spirit of neutrality, which is the spirit of impartiality and fairness and friendliness to all concerned. The spirit of the nation in this critical matter will be determined largely by what individuals and society and those gathered in public meetings do and say, upon what newspapers and magazines contain, upon what ministers utter in their pulpits, and [what] men proclaim as their opinions upon the street."

As proof that his words were sincere, Wilson sent Colonel House to Europe in an attempt to resolve disagreements between the Allies and Central powers. He also encouraged the public not to display support for one European country over another. The president advised the American people to instead be impartial and demonstrate intelligence as they kept themselves informed of fighting overseas. As the war progressed, however, Germany's actions made it increasingly difficult for Wilson and his fellow Americans to maintain this attitude.

Fighting for Neutrality and Finding New Love

While the president of the United States urged his countrymen to remain neutral, Britain and Germany struggled for control on the

Atlantic Ocean. The British navy captured any merchant ships that it suspected might deliver food or military supplies to Central troops. Essentially, the British hoped to blockade Germany—that is, prevent it from receiving supplies or reinforcements.

Yet the Germans were determined to overcome the blockade. Thus, instead of simply taking control of British ships, they began to attack them with torpedoes. Though many Americans criticized Germany's failure to give passengers or crews aboard these vessels a chance to escape, Wilson continued to urge the people to stay as impartial as possible. Even he, however, could not remain silent when a British luxury liner called the *Lusitania* sank off the coast of Ireland after being torpedoed by a German submarine on May 7, 1915.

On May 7, 1915, the British ship the Lusitania *sank as a result of a torpedo hit by a German submarine.*

The sinking of the *Lusitania* resulted in more than a thousand deaths—including 128 Americans. Wilson was furious and wasted no time in instructing his secretary of state, William Jennings Bryan, to draft a formal protest. He promptly demanded that the Central powers put a halt to actions that would in any way threaten the lives of U.S. citizens. Part of the protest read as follows: "The [German] government will not expect the government of the United States to omit any word or any act necessary to the performance of its sacred duty of maintaining the rights of the United States and its citizens and of safeguarding their free exercise and enjoyment."

After several months of negotiations, Germany reluctantly responded by promising that it would not target passenger ships or vessels controlled by neutral nations. In turn, Wilson continued to ask the American people to stay calm and impartial. "The example of America must be the example not merely of peace because it will not fight, but of peace because it is the healing and elevating influence of the world. . . . There is such a thing as a man being too proud to fight. There is such a thing as a nation being so right that it does not need to convince others by force that it is right."

Despite the eloquence of Wilson's words, however, U.S. citizens would have a reason to question them in the years ahead. By 1916 Germany was violating the agreement it had made with the United States about giving adequate warning to enemy ships before launching torpedo attacks. Wilson repeated his protests to German officials, and they once more vowed to observe the agreement. Nevertheless, the U.S. president remained watchful and tense, realizing that it was growing harder and harder to keep his country neutral in the conflict overseas.

Fortunately, by that time the president's personal life was improving. Although completely devastated by Ellen Wilson's death, he had had few private moments to grieve before being thrown into the unfolding drama of World War I. Between losing his wife and having to respond to disaster in Europe, he was in desperate need of someone who could provide him with support, friendship, and a reminder that it was still possible for happiness to exist in his world. A widowed friend of Wilson's cousin offered him these things and more. Edith Bolling Galt, who first met the president in the spring of 1915, instantly captivated him with her lively, independent spirit. Yet some of Wilson's friends and advisers thought the romance was moving

An Ideal Companion

After months of deep depression related to the death of his precious Ellen, Wilson found comfort in his relationship with Edith Bolling Galt. Considered by those around her to be both charming and attractive, she was filled with the very spirit the president seemed to have lost after the death of Ellen. "You are so vivid. . . . You are so beautiful!" he wrote to his new friend not long after they met. "I have learned what you are, and my heart is wholly enthralled. You are my ideal companion. . . . The old shadows are gone, the old loneliness banished, the new joy let in like a great healing light. I feel, when I think of the wonderful happiness that your love has brought me, a new faith in everything that is fine and full of hope."

Charming and lively, Edith Bolling Galt won Wilson's heart not long after they met.

along too fast. Ellen had passed away less than a year before Wilson was introduced to Edith, and his supporters worried that a prompt second marriage would be seen as inappropriate by voters in the upcoming election of 1916.

The president understood this but was also forced to admit that he had been completely won over by the new love in his life. Wilson therefore pushed ahead with a wedding in December 1915. As he joyfully looked forward to life with his second wife, he also began planning to win a second term in the White House during an international crisis that did not appear to be nearing an end.

Fighting for Four More Years

Even though Wilson had asked Congress to provide funds to strengthen the nation's armed forces in 1915, he insisted during the 1916 presidential campaign that he would continue to do everything possible to prevent U.S. involvement in overseas fighting. His supporters proudly displayed the campaign slogan "He kept us out of war" and also pointed to the many Progressive reforms that the president had accomplished during his first four years in office.

Yet Wilson still faced a far greater challenge in winning the race for the White House than he had in 1912. One of the main reasons for this was that the Republican Party had learned from its mistakes in the previous election. The leaders of the opposition realized that they could not possibly achieve victory if they remained divided. The majority of Republicans were in agreement that former chief justice of the United States Charles Evans Hughes was a strong candidate who, with the full support of his party, stood the best chance of defeating Wilson.

Wilson knew he had to fight a fierce campaign to win a second term in office in 1916.

Unlike Hughes, however, the president did not have the luxury of focusing all his energy on the campaign. The war in Europe was forever on his mind, and, in the spring of 1916, problems in Mexico again required his close attention. At about that time, revolutionary leader Pancho Villa had carried out a raid in Columbus, New Mexico, which had resulted in the death of seventeen Americans. The Mexican rebel leader was eager to force the United States into war in the hope that Venustiano Carranza would be overthrown in the unstable situation sure to result from a declared war.

Wilson did not take Villa's bait, but he *did* send troops into northern Mexico to hunt down the rebel forces. Unfortunately, the U.S. soldiers, commanded by General John J. Pershing failed to capture the bandit chief. While Wilson had kept America out of war with Mexico, his opponents in the 1916 election were able to point out that he had also failed to locate Villa.

Ultimately, though, voters granted the president another term. Not everyone agreed with his policies, but most U.S. citizens were grateful that he had helped them avoid being swept up in the danger and destruction of global war. While Wilson could not claim an overwhelming victory, he could still tell Americans in November 1916 that he would proudly serve as their leader for another four years. When the final results were tallied, approximately 9.1 million voters and 277 members of the electoral college had cast ballots in his favor. In comparison, Hughes had received the backing of 8.5 million citizens and 254 electors. Thus, whatever satisfaction Wilson took in winning, he understood that the moment was hardly right for confident celebration.

"Let us remember," he told his supporters in November 1916, "now that the campaign is over, to get together for the common good of all." Americans would need to hear this reminder again in the days ahead. For, within months of his reelection, Wilson would guide the United States into the heat of battle across the Atlantic Ocean.

*G*ermany's promises to Woodrow Wilson were not honored for long. Two months after the president was reelected, his counterpart, German emperor Wilhelm II, returned to the same tactics that had prompted the president to send warnings to Central powers starting in 1915. German commanders were now determined to blockade Great Britain, which continued to receive boatloads of food and supplies from America. In order to starve the British and rob them of military reinforcements, Germany once again began using submarines to launch torpedo attacks.

Realizing that this pattern of warfare would inevitably affect

A political cartoon depicts Wilson shoving a boulder with the words "Foreign Complications" up a hill; the president indeed faced several overseas complications not long after his re-election.

U.S. ships traveling to Great Britain, Wilson accepted that it was time to end all diplomatic relations with Germany. This meant that the United States would no longer negotiate with German officials or have any formal dealings with representatives of that country. Wilson announced his plans in early February 1917.

Within weeks, Americans had a reason to applaud his decision. The reason came in the form of a coded telegram sent by Arthur Zimmermann, Germany's foreign minister, to his country's ambassador in Mexico.

Zimmermann's telegram fell into the hands of the British, who decoded it and learned that the ambassador had been directed to create an alliance with Mexican officials that would involve plotting against the United States. The foreign secretary went so far as to express the hope that Mexico would be willing to attack American troops along the border if the U.S. Congress formally declared war on Germany. Zimmermann also noted that, in exchange for this display of loyalty toward Central forces, the Germans would help Mexico recover the states of Texas and New Mexico when their victory was complete.

German politician Arthur Zimmermann authored a telegram that heightened American hostility toward Germany.

The contents of the message, which were revealed to the public in early March 1917, increased U.S. hostility toward the Central powers. In addition, U.S. fury at the Zimmermann telegram was mingled with fear and concern about how the war was progressing in Europe. Russia, which had been one of the Allies, was by the spring of 1917 in the throes of revolution. The czar, or emperor, had been forced to give up his power, and the government was in a state of chaos.

Suddenly free from serious challenges on the Russian front, German forces swarmed west toward France. The British and French were faced with the very real possibility of being overrun by their enemies if they did not receive immediate military assistance. Recognizing this, Wilson acknowledged that U.S. neutrality was no longer an option. He believed that international democracy was at stake if America did not act. On April 2, 1917, the president therefore appealed to Congress to formally declare war on Germany.

On April 2 1917, Wilson asked Congress to declare war on Germany.

"It is a war against all nations," he emphasized. "American ships have been sunk, [and] American lives taken in ways which it has stirred us very deeply to learn of, but the ships and people of other neutral and friendly nations have been sunk and overwhelmed in the waters in the same way. There has been no discrimination. The challenge is to all mankind. Each nation must decide for itself how it will meet it. . . . The world must be made safe for democracy."

In the end, Congress agreed with Wilson. U.S. legislators declared war on Germany not long after he asked them to do so. Wilson, however, was fully aware that the path to making the entire world safe for democracy would not be easy, nor would it be without enormous costs to Americans everywhere.

"It is a fearful thing to lead this great, peaceful people into war, into the most terrible and disastrous of all wars, civilization itself seeming to be in the balance," he reflected. For the next year, he and his countrymen would indeed have to face some of their worst fears and their most overwhelming challenges. Yet, with Wilson's guidance, they would also take tremendous steps toward achieving world peace.

In the Trenches and on the Home Front

Once the United States formally entered World War I, life changed drastically both for the soldiers who served in the U.S. military and for the civilians who remained on America's home front. Approximately 2.5 million men were instructed to report for duty in response to a draft that Congress adopted in May 1917. A draft is an official order that calls upon individuals to enlist in the military—regardless of whether they want to.

A poster calling on Americans to register for the draft in 1917.

As American commanders trained these servicemen, they also worked closely with Wilson and U.S. congressmen. The president participated in countless discussions that dealt with topics such as funding the war, manufacturing military supplies, and transporting troops overseas. Wilson was aware that every decision he made required extremely careful consideration since American lives were at stake.

At the same time, however, he realized that he also had to act as quickly as possible. Allied forces were growing weary and overwhelmed after nearly three years of battle. Troops in France were beginning to mutiny, or rebel, and Russia was almost entirely out of the picture.

The first wave of American soldiers, which arrived on European shores in July 1917, started engaging in trench warfare in October. World War I was famous for this type of combat, in which enemy forces attacked each other from long ditches that had been dug in the ground. The fighting was bloody and difficult. Before the war ended in 1918, at least 116,516 U.S. troops would be killed while serving their country.

World War I was famous for both sides engaging in trench warfare.

Yet Wilson's challenges were not limited to making decisions about American soldiers in European trenches. He understood that the war was destined to take a toll on the home front, as well. Men, women, and children were frightened by the deadly possibilities that the conflict represented. People worried about their friends and relatives overseas, and many experienced rage and hatred for anyone of German descent—even those who were patriotic U.S. citizens. Indeed, before Wilson had asked Congress for a formal declaration of war, he had expressed the fear that it would have tragic consequences for the American people:

[War] would mean that we should lose our heads along with the rest and stop weighing right and wrong. . . . Once lead this people into war, and they'll forget there ever was such a thing as tolerance. To fight, you must be brutal and ruthless, and the spirit of ruthless brutality will enter into the very fiber of our national life, infecting Congress, the courts, the policemen on the beat, [and] the man in the street."

Wilson's prediction sadly proved true. Anyone who was suspected of unpatriotic activities such as spying or avoiding the draft might be imprisoned or forced to pay a hefty fine as a result of the Espionage Act, which was passed by the U.S. Congress in June 1917. Suspicion and terror tore apart once peaceful communities across the country. Some Americans lashed out with physical violence against foreigners and pacifists, or people who were against the war.

Nevertheless, the conflict overseas had some positive effects on U.S. citizens on the home front. Whenever possible, Wilson did what he could to unify members of the public as part of the war effort. For example, he oversaw programs that helped make sure industry and agriculture did not suffer because factory workers and farmers had been drafted to fight in Europe.

The president also encouraged Americans to conserve, or save, their resources. Avoiding waste was especially important because of the diminished labor force on the home front and the requirement for a steady stream of supplies for U.S. soldiers in Europe. At one point the government went beyond attacking waste and urged sacrifice, suggesting that citizens choose a different day each week on which they would not eat certain items, such as meat and bread.

A Controversial Committee

In April 1917, Wilson created what became known as the Committee on Public Information (CPI). The president established this government agency to raise public awareness and support of American involvement in World War I. Members of the CPI used newspapers, posters, radio, cinema, and other media outlets to boost U.S. patriotism.

The committee often stirred fear and anger, as well, however. CPI artwork sometimes depicted Germans as monsters or showed enemy soldiers murdering small children. The campaign also caused certain members of the public to become overly suspicious of German Americans, who frequently experienced harassment and humiliation or were forced to prove their loyalty by dramatic displays, such as kissing the American flag.

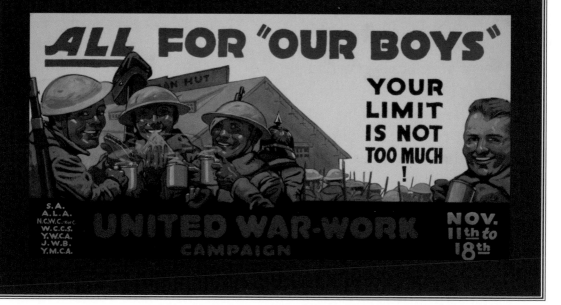

This 1918 poster encourages Americans to conserve various food resources during World War I.

Perhaps most importantly, however, Wilson was determined that the nation have clear goals about what it hoped to accomplish by being involved in the war. He did not want American lives to be spent in vain, and he did not want U.S. citizens to view the conflict simply as a way to get revenge or murder the enemy. So, the president arranged for a special meeting of Congress on January 8, 1918, and delivered what would become known as his Fourteen Points speech.

During this address, Wilson specifically outlined what America wanted to achieve by going to war. By overcoming the Central powers and their threat to democracy, he believed that the United States could play a major role in promoting long-term international peace. Wilson described fourteen ways in which this could be accomplished, including working toward more open relationships among various governments. He also proposed that fairer trade agreements be established, that nations gradually reduce their production of weapons, and that when the war reached its end, the borders of several European countries be more clearly defined.

Yet it was the fourteenth point for which Wilson is probably best remembered. The president suggested that "a general association of nations must be formed under specific covenants for the purpose of affording mutual guarantees of political independence and territorial

President Woodrow Wilson addressed Congress in 1918 proposing the end of World War I.

integrity to great and small states alike." Put another way, Wilson wanted to create an organization that would allow governments to more effectively work together and communicate better with each another. Ultimately, he believed that the new international body, which later came to exist as the **League of Nations**, would also help people across the globe avoid the horrors of another war like the one they were still desperately trying to survive throughout most of 1918.

HOPE AFTER THE HORROR OF WAR

As the year progressed, things began to look up for the Allied powers. With the "Yanks," or American troops, on their side, Great Britain and France were better positioned to fight German forces. Gradually, a greater number of German soldiers started to mutiny, and, on November 9, 1918, Kaiser Wilhelm II gave up his power.

The front page of The Los Angeles Times, *October 13, 1918, announces the German's acceptance of peace established by President Wilson.*

Within days, Germany asked for an **armistice**, or ceasefire, that would allow the heads of government of the belligerent nations, the participants in the war, to arrange peace talks. Representatives of the Allied powers agreed to this request on November 11, 1918. For all purposes, World War I was at an end. Some experts believe that approximately 37 million people were killed, wounded, or reported missing during the course of the conflict.

Nearly everyone who had played any significant role in the fighting was exhausted and extremely relieved that the bloodshed was at long last over. Many people also regarded Wilson as a hero both for his decision to involve America in the war and for his dedication to creating stability and peace once the last bullet had been fired. As news of the armistice with Germany spread, he was repeatedly greeted with congratulations and gratitude.

"I thank you and the people of the United States for the high and noble part which you have played in this glorious chapter of history," declared King George V of Britain. At the same time, however, national leaders and average men and women alike were experiencing mixed emotions. They looked to the future with fear, hope, and a desire to move ahead, never to repeat the disaster that had begun in 1914.

In less than five years of fighting, the world had been drastically changed. People everywhere had new perspectives on what war meant. They also had a deep interest in achieving long lasting peace—just as Wilson discussed during his Fourteen Points speech. Seeing the armistice as an opportunity to achieve his goals for international unity, the president eagerly prepared to participate in a peace conference scheduled to begin in December 1918.

Unlike U.S. leaders before him, Wilson did not send an ambassador to speak for him at this important meeting. Rather, becoming the first president to sail across Atlantic waters while in office, he would journey to Paris with his wife and several advisers and government officials. He was exhausted from the strain that the events of the past year had placed on him, but he was excited and optimistic, as well.

Wilson told U.S. citizens who listened to his annual State of the Union address in December 1918 that he hoped to return to them soon "with the happy assurance" that he had been able "to translate into action the great ideals for which America has striven." Winning this assurance would not come easily, however, nor without a price to his own well-being. Just as stubborn and unwilling to compromise as he had been during his days as president of Princeton, Wilson would soon prove equally determined when it came to creating a better world exactly as he envisioned it.

A BITTERSWEET GOODBYE TO AMERICA *Eight*

Woodrow Wilson had great plans to promote the League of Nations when he arrived in Paris in late 1918. Yet he quickly learned that not every world leader present shared his ambitions. Achieving international peace and unity were certainly noble goals, but many of the men attending the conference in France had other concerns.

President Woodrow Wilson traveled to Paris in 1918 to discuss preliminary terms of peace.

A portrait of Wilson (seated, third from left) and other international leaders during peace negotiations in Paris.

European countries had been torn apart by a long and costly war, and their leaders were anxious to rebuild their governments and economies, as well as to establish new national boundaries. Wilson's ideas regarding the league were therefore met with admiration but were not taken very seriously. He had grand thoughts for the future, but European heads of states were pre-occupied with more immediate situations.

When Wilson returned home in February 1919, he confidently left Colonel House in France to continue to participate in peace discussions. Much to the president's disappointment, however, House failed to stand firm on several of Wilson's key issues. For starters, he showed approval for policies that required the defeated Central powers to pay to Allies huge sums of money, called reparations. These payments were intended to compensate victorious countries for damages they had suffered during the war. In addition, House supported the notion of dividing

Wilson appeared much older and frail by the end of his presidency.

governor James M. Cox as their candidate for the 1920 race.

Yet it was the Republican nominee, Warren G. Harding, who ultimately claimed victory in the election. Countless Americans applauded Wilson's efforts, but just as many felt the nation was ready for change. The public had spent years hearing about the president's dreams for a League of Nations and were no longer as deeply inspired by Progressive ideals. Harding's campaign slogan promising a "return to normalcy" offered greater appeal to U.S. voters, who wanted just that after experiencing the devastation of World War I.

About four months before leaving office, Wilson was awarded the Nobel Peace Prize in acknowledgment of his extraordinary efforts toward creating international unity. Wilson was honored because of his role in promoting the League of Nations, but his sense of achievement after being named a Nobel

winner was somewhat bittersweet. After all, the United States was not able to play a part in the organization he had fought so hard to establish.

It was with similarly mixed emotions that, in March 1921, Wilson bid farewell to the White House and the weighty responsibilities of leadership. He watched Harding

Wilson riding with president-elect Warren G. Harding to the latter's inauguration at the U.S. Capitol in Washington, D.C., March 4, 1921

sworn into office and then retreated to a home that he and Edith had purchased in Washington, D.C. Although by this time he had overcome the more serious effects of his stroke, those around him noticed that, as he aged, he grew forgetful and short-tempered. By late 1923, he was sixty-seven years old, but he still talked about possibly running in the presidential election the following year. His family and friends—and the Democratic Party—recognized, however, that this was a completely impractical ambition.

Wilson had never fully recovered from his stroke, and his health continued to decline up until the early winter of 1924. Then, on February 3 of that year, the man who had faithfully served as the twenty-eighth president of the United States died in his home in the nation's capital. Wilson's remains lie in a tomb in Washington's National Cathedral.

An American Leader's Legacy

Nearly a hundred years after he made his way to the White House, Wilson continues to be remembered for his contributions to the country. He earned a reputation for fighting corruption both in politics and in some of the nation's biggest businesses. Wilson also became known for supporting financial and labor policies that he believed went hand in hand with the ideals of the Progressive movement and were likely to benefit average Americans who worked for a living.

Perhaps most importantly, however, he earned a place in history for attempting to keep the United States out of World War I—and for leading U.S. citizens through that deadly and life-changing conflict when neutrality became impossible. People continue to respect and admire his efforts toward international peace decades after he fought to see them achieved, even if Wilson himself thought he had failed when it came to the League of Nations.

As an American and the president of the United States, Wilson described himself as an idealist. As a young man, he was deeply committed to helping shape a more perfect country, and he never abandoned that goal, regardless of whether he was heading Princeton University or acting as governor of New Jersey. By the time he was elected to the nation's highest office, he already had a

ANOTHER ATTITUDE REGARDING SUFFRAGE

By 1918, Wilson appeared to have experienced a shift in attitude regarding the suffrage movement. In January of that year, he publicly declared his support for a change to the U.S. Constitution that would guarantee women across the country the right to vote in national elections. Though it would be more than two years before the Nineteenth Amendment was officially adopted, Wilson continued to argue with Congress in favor of suffrage in the meantime.

His opinions were undoubtedly altered in part by the amazing contributions female citizens had made during World War I. While men were fighting overseas, women did everything from running families to maintaining industry by taking jobs in factories. "We have made partners of the women in this war," he observed during one speech to Congress in 1918, "Shall we admit them only to a partnership of suffering and sacrifice and toil and not to a partnership of privilege and right?"

remarkable appreciation for the duties and responsibilities that he understood would fill his days in the White House.

Yet Wilson was by no means perfect. He did not always treat women or African Americans fairly. In addition, he often proved overly stubborn in situations that might have been resolved better or more quickly if he had been willing to compromise.

Thomas Woodrow Wilson made up for a few notable character flaws by displaying intelligence and dedication. He faced great challenges during his lifetime—both on a personal and professional level—but he always attempted to put America first. Not everyone agreed with his opinions or decisions, but no one questioned his integrity or doubted his conviction that his positions represented the best interests of U.S. citizens.

"America was established . . . to realize a vision," Wilson once remarked. "To realize an ideal—to discover and maintain liberty among men." The twenty-eighth president of the United States spent much of his career working to help his countrymen transform this ideal into a reality. Future generations might continue to debate his level of success, but few people can question his commitment to trying.

Wilson's legacy continues to be remembered in American politics and history several decades after his death.

1856
Born December 28 in
Staunton, Virginia

1879
Graduates from the College
of New Jersey, later renamed
Princeton University

1885
Weds Ellen Axson in June

1902
Is appointed president of
Princeton University

1910
Is elected governor of New
Jersey

1912
Wins the Democratic
nomination for president
and claims victory in the
November election

1850

1915
Marries Edith Bolling Galt
in December

1916
Is elected to a second term in
the White House

1918
Delivers the Fourteen
Points speech

1920
Is awarded the Nobel
Peace Prize for efforts
toward promoting
international unity

1924
Dies at his home in the
nation's capital on
February 3

1930

NOTES

CHAPTER 1

p. 7, ". . . people call me an idealist . . .": quoted in "About Woodrow Wilson: Famous Quotations," the Woodrow Wilson International Center for Scholars, www.wilsoncenter.org/index.cfm?fuseaction=about.woodrow#quotes (accessed August 26, 2009).

p. 10, ". . . even at the age of . . .": quoted in Woodrow Wilson, *National Historic Landmark Nomination*, www.nps.gov/history/nhl/Fall07Nominations/Wilson%20Boyhood%20Home.pdf (accessed August 24, 2009).

p. 11, "extremely dignified . . . not like other boys . . .": quoted in Sigmund Freud and William C. Bullitt, *Woodrow Wilson: A Psychological Study*. (New Brunswick, NJ: Transaction, 1999, p. 6).

p. 16, ". . . consequence of the excitement . . .": quoted in August Heckscher, *Woodrow Wilson*. (New York: Scribner's, 1991, p. 35).

p. 17, ". . . profession I chose was . . .": quoted in Freud and Bullitt, *Woodrow Wilson*, p. 22.

CHAPTER 2

p. 18, ". . . terribly bored by the noble . . .": quoted in Freud and Bullitt, *Woodrow Wilson*, p. 22.

p. 21, ". . . only person in the world . . .": quoted in Freud and Bullitt, *Woodrow Wilson*, p. 25.

p. 25, ". . . young women of the present . . .": quoted in Anne Firor Scott and Andrew MacKay Scott, *One Half the People: The Fight for Woman Suffrage*. (Urbana: University of Illinois Press, 1982, p. 149).

p. 26, ". . . had a contagious interest . . .": quoted in Heckscher, *Woodrow Wilson*, pp. 94–95.

p. 26, ". . . talked to us in the most . . .": quoted in Heckscher, *Woodrow Wilson*, p. 95.

p. 26, ". . . it seems to me . . .": Woodrow Wilson, "Princeton in the Nation's Service" (date last updated not available), Princeton University, Almagest, http://etcweb.princeton.edu/CampusWWW/Companion/princeton_in_nations_service.html (accessed August 24, 2009).

CHAPTER 3

p. 29, ". . . life-long friend and companion": quoted in Heckscher, *Woodrow Wilson*, p. 141.

p. 30, ". . . want to transform thoughtless boys . . .": Woodrow Wilson, "New Ideas for Princeton," *New York Times* (December 10, 1902), http://query.nytimes.com/mem/archive-free/pdf?_r=1&res=9403EFD81E3DEE32A25753C1A9649D946397D6CF (accessed August 24, 2009).

p. 33, ". . . the fact that a new day . . .": James Chace, *1912: Wilson, Roosevelt, Taft & Debs: The Election That Changed the Country.* (New York: Simon & Schuster, 2004, p. 52).

p. 34, "revival of the power of the people": quoted in Chace, *1912*, p. 52.

p. 35, ". . . personal magnetism of the man . . .": quoted in Chace, *1912*, p. 53.

CHAPTER 4

p. 37, ". . . ingrate and a liar": quoted in Alexander L. George and Juliette L. George, *Woodrow Wilson and Colonel House: A Personality Study.* (New York: Dover Publications, 1964, p. 72).

p. 38, ". . . ends its session with the most . . .": quoted in Heckscher, *Woodrow Wilson,* p. 227.

p. 38, ". . . quietly and deeply happy . . .": quoted in Heckscher, *Woodrow Wilson,* p. 227.

p. 41, ". . . they seem to like me . . .": quoted in Heckscher, *Woodrow Wilson,* p. 235.

p. 44, ". . . next president of the United States . . .": quoted in Heckscher, *Woodrow Wilson,* p. 253.

p. 46, ". . . feeling of solemn responsibility . . .": quoted in Heckscher, *Woodrow Wilson,* p. 263.

CHAPTER 5

p. 48, ". . . not a day of . . .": quoted in Heckscher, *Woodrow Wilson,* p. 274.

p. 55, ". . . art and practice of government consists not . . .": Woodrow Wilson, "Wilson's Address at the Woman Suffrage Convention, Atlantic City, NJ, September 8, 1916," *President Wilson's State Papers and Addresses* (New York: Review of Reviews Company, 1918, p. 237).

p. 56, ". . . purpose of these measures . . .": Woodrow Wilson, *Wilson: A Portrait—African Americans* (specific date last updated not available), PBS, http://www.pbs.org/wgbh/amex/wilson/portrait/wp_african.html (accessed August 25, 2009).

p. 59, ". . . has stricken me almost beyond . . .": quoted in Heckscher, *Woodrow Wilson,* p. 334.

GLOSSARY

Allied forces a group of nations (that initially included Britain, France, Belgium, Serbia, Montenegro, and Russia) that opposed Central forces during World War I

armistice a cease-fire that gives nations at war an opportunity to discuss possible terms of peace

cabinet the group of politicians who advise a leader such as the president and head various government departments

Central powers a group of nations (that initially included Germany and Austria-Hungary) that opposed Allied forces during World War I

checks and balances a system for preventing any one of the three branches of the U.S. government from becoming too powerful; means to this end include the veto and the amendment

Democrat a member of one of the two major political parties in the United States who, especially in Wilson's era, tended to back reform and other progressive policies

dyslexia a learning disability that often makes it difficult for people to view written letters in the correct order

electoral college a group of people consisting of representatives from every state and Washington, D.C., who cast their votes for the U.S. president and vice president after the results for the general election have been tallied

House of Representatives one of two legislative bodies that make up the U.S. Congress, the other being the Senate

League of Nations an international organization formed in 1920 to encourage long-term world peace; in 1946 it was dissolved and replaced by the United Nations

legislature a government body that has the power to make, change, or repeal laws

machine politics a system in which leaders called bosses head political organizations and exert strict control over the members of the group or party they oversee; bosses often reward their supporters with political offices and are sometimes involved in corrupt practices

monopolies exclusive or near exclusive providers of products or services that many buyers or people desire

parliament the lawmaking body of Great Britain

primaries early elections in which voters choose candidates to represent their geographic area or political party in a later race for a certain office

Progressive movement a political movement that gained recognition in the late 1800s and early 1900s; Progressives called for stricter government regulation of businesses and utilities, increased workers' rights, and a greater voice for U.S. voters in political affairs

Republican a member of one of the two major political parties in the United States; especially in Wilson's era, Republicans tended to be less open to new ideas and more in favor of traditional policies

secretary of state the member of the president's cabinet who oversees foreign relations

secretary of the treasury the member of the president's cabinet who oversees the Department of the Treasury and is the president's chief economic adviser

Senate one of two legislative bodies that make up the U.S. Congress, the other being the House of Representatives

FirstWorldWar.com

www.firstworldwar.com/

A site with extensive information about World War I, including the role that Wilson played in this conflict.

PBS American Experience: Woodrow Wilson

www.pbs.org/wgbh/amex/wilson/

A collection of online resources that features a timeline and biographical data on Wilson.

The Woodrow Wilson Presidential Library

www.woodrowwilson.org/

A site with a detailed overview of the Woodrow Wilson Museum, as well as a series of online documents related to Wilson's presidency.

BIBLIOGRAPHY

BOOKS

Chace, James. *1912: Wilson, Roosevelt, Taft & Debs: The Election That Changed the Country* New York: Simon & Schuster, 2004.

Freud, Sigmund, and William C. Bullitt. *Woodrow Wilson: A Psychological Study*. New Brunswick, NJ: Transaction, 1999.

George, Alexander L., and Juliette L. George. *Woodrow Wilson and Colonel House: A Personality Study*. New York: Dover, 1964.

Heckscher, August. *Woodrow Wilson*. New York: Scribner's, 1991.

———, ed. *The Politics of Woodrow Wilson: Selections from His Speeches and Writings*. Freeport, NY: Books for Libraries Press, 1970.

Maynard, W. Barksdale. *Woodrow Wilson: Princeton to the Presidency*. New Haven, CT: Yale University Press, 2008.

President Wilson's State Papers and Addresses. New York: Review of Reviews Company, 1918.

Scott, Anne Firor, and Andrew MacKay Scott. *One Half the People: The Fight for Woman Suffrage*. Urbana: University of Illinois Press, 1982.

DVD

Woodrow Wilson. Directed by Carl Byker and Mitchell Wilson, 2007. Originally broadcast in 2002 in the *American Experience* Series (PBS).

★ ★ ★ ★ ★ ★ ★ ★ ★ ★ ★ ★ ★ ★ ★ ★ ★

INDEX

Pages in **boldface** are illustrations.

ABOUT THE AUTHOR

Katie Marsico is the author of more than sixty reference books for children and young adults. Prior to becoming a full-time writer, Ms. Marsico worked as a managing editor in publishing. She resides near Chicago, Illinois, with her husband, daughter, and two sons.